Alan Stibbs has an irresistible argument here, and it is one that is essential for Christian assurance. Where this message rings out, be sure to see pastoral comfort, be sure to hear cries of 'Hallelujah! What a Saviour!'

Michael Reeves
Head of Theology, UCCF

At a time when liberalism dominated the church and the classroom in the UK, Alan Stibbs' voice spoke out clearly for an intelligent and passionate statement of the truth of the gospel. After a stint on the mission field he returned to the UK and alongside Martyn Lloyd-Jones and John Stott provided leadership for the growing reformed and evangelical movement. As a theological student I discovered Stibbs' writings and found in them a reasoned and winsome defense of biblical Christianity. Nowhere is this more in evidence than in this small work on the Atonement. With utter clarity he identifies the main issues involved in a biblical understanding of the cross. Here is a biblical and reasoned defense of the teaching on the blood of Christ. Often underused in our drive for relevance and cultural acceptance we cannot escape the NT's typical reference to Jesus sacrifice in terms of his precious blood shed for sinners. You will want to read this little booklet and refresh your spirit by drinking from this rich supply of living water. It is a miniature treasure.

Liam Goligher
Senior Pastor, Tenth Presbyterian Church,
Philadelphia, Pennsylvania

Solid gold! Alan Stibb's brilliant study of "the meaning of the word 'blood' in Scripture" is one of those classics that has directly or indirectly influenced generations of Bible readers. The errors that Stibbs was combatting decades ago may not be exactly the same as today's challenges to a Biblical understanding of the death of Jesus, but his exposition is just what we need. Why does the Bible speak so frequently of the blood of Christ? What did Jesus mean by "drink my blood"? What did Paul mean by "participation in the blood of Christ"? Pursue these questions with Alan Stibbs as your guide and you will deepen your appreciation of God's grace and your salvation, both focussed in the sacrificial death of our Lord Jesus Christ.

John Woodhouse
Principal, Moore College, Sydney

For Stibbs, though, the Cross remains central. He will not let us forget the magnitude of the guilt-cleansing benefits of Jesus' death for his people. It is precisely on the themes of the greatness of Jesus' offering and the greatness of our sin against him that Stibbs ends his essay. On the one hand, Stibbs' essay is a theological jewel, with its close and lucid reading of biblical material. On the other hand, it is a pastoral masterpiece, because the reader loves Christ more at the end of it. I think that would greatly please Alan Stibbs, and it is why this 'old' essay is so worth reading.

Michael Ovey
Principal, Doctrine, Apologetics & Liturgy,
Oakhill College, London

HIS
BLOOD
WORKS

The Meaning of the word 'Blood' in Scripture

ALAN STIBBS

CHRISTIAN
HERITAGE

Scripture quotations are taken, unless otherwise stated, from the Authorised Version (AV). Other quotations are from the Revised Version (RV).

ISBN 978-1-84550-726-8

10 9 8 7 6 5 4 3 2 1

First published in 1962 as *The Meaning of the word 'Blood' in Scripture*. It was originally a chapter in Alan Stibbs' *Such a Great Salvation* (ISBN 978-1-84550-423-6)
Reprinted in 2011
by
Christian Focus Publications,
Geanies House, Fearn, Ross-shire,
IV20 1TW, Scotland, United Kingdom

www.christianfocus.com

Cover design by Daniel van Straaten
Printed by Nørhaven, Denmark

CONTENTS

Foreword by *Michael Ovey* 7

Introduction 19

1. Examination of Scriptural Usage
   in the Old Testament 33

2. Examination of Scriptural Usage
   in the New Testament 49

Conclusion 77

Foreword

Does Alan Stibbs' essay 'His Blood Works' count as old? By the standards of modern scholarship it does, because it was first published in 1962, and since then much has been written about sacrifice in the Old Testament and about the atonement that Jesus Christ offers. In such thinking the word 'old' suggests 'out-dated' and 'out-moded'.

In a consumerist society it is fatal for a product to attract the tag 'old' in that sense, and it is worth bearing in mind that Christian readers and Christian academics can have consumerist attitudes too. Part of the sadness about a consumerist society is its difficulty in finding contentment and rest, because it consistently demands more: it is insatiable, and this marches very closely with what older generations called gluttony.

It is possible for Christians, whether academics or not, to have an intellectual gluttony which is equally insatiable, not in the sense simply of searching to learn, but rather looking for something new for the sake simply of the newness. We rightly decry a merely entertainment culture in public worship in churches, where a church service looks like a cross between a game show and a pop concert, precisely because it takes so much so uncritically from a worldly entertainment consumerism. We sometimes forget that consumerism can be there on the bookshelf too. Such a consumerist attitude will, I think, tend to dismiss Stibbs and his essay.

That would be a great loss. For the word 'old' can have other connotations than 'outdated'. 'Old' can suggest 'old master', and it can suggest wisdom. Like so much of his work, Stibbs' *His Blood Works* is old in that sense. C.S. Lewis wrote of the value of reading old works because of their enduring value; a characteristic simplicity; and their ability to address us in our limited horizons because, while products of their own times, they are not captured by the spirit of our times in the way that we are.[1] All these characteristics are present in 'His Blood Works'.

Stibbs' essential case can be summarised fairly shortly: it is highly important to work out what the word 'blood' means in the Bible because the work of Jesus Christ is so frequently referred to in terms of his blood. This means that our understanding of 'blood' affects our understanding of the Cross. The word 'blood' in the Bible, Stibbs argues, does not stand for life released for new purposes, but does stand for the benefits given by the life laid down in death.[2]

At first hearing, one is tempted to ask what the difference is between these two accounts of what 'blood' means and why it matters. After all, some would say that the idea of 'life released for new purposes' does not deny that Jesus Christ died, nor that his death was necessary, nor that it was sufficient. However part of Stibbs' enduring value is that he does see a difference and he explains its significance with such clarity. He penetratingly asks

---

1   C.S. Lewis, 'Introduction', pp 3-10 in *St Athanasius On the Incarnation*. St Vladimir's Seminary Press: Crestwood NY, 1993 (original edition 1944).

2   See for example Stibbs' summary of the Old Testament evidence on p 35 of this edition and his reference to the drinking language of John 6:54-58 on p 61.

whether the necessity and sufficiency of Christ's death really is the same in the two different accounts of what 'blood' means.

The way Stibbs structures the argument in four short sections helps readers see this very clearly. Thus, he explains in his introduction why the definition of 'blood' matters and where the idea of 'blood' as 'life released' principally comes from, namely B. F. Westcott's commentary on 1 John published in 1883.[3]

He then develops in chapter 1 an account of the range of what 'blood' means in the Old Testament, in the course of which he shows why the three major texts apparently in favour of the 'life released' case (Gen. 9:4, Lev. 17:11 and Deut. 12:23) do not support this reading when examined more closely in context.[4] Stibbs summarises: 'Blood shed stands, therefore, not for the release of life from the burden of the flesh, but for the bringing to an end of life in the flesh.'[5]

Chapter 2 is, naturally, an account of New Testament usage, showing how 'blood' is associated with the benefits of a life laid down in death, while the conclusion develops

---

3   See p 14. Westcott was commenting on 1 John 4:8.

4   See p 25.

5   See p 26.

the magnitude both of our plight and our redemption when 'blood' is viewed as referring to the death of Christ in its redemptive significance.[6]

Why, then, was it so important for Stibbs to refute Westcott's case about 'life released'? The answer lies in the way that Westcott's view can lead to an anaemic view of the Cross (if the pun can be excused) which understates key aspects of the saving work of Christ.

Critically, the idea of 'blood' as the release of life for new purposes tends to divorce the shedding of blood from the idea of sin involving the penalty of death, both physical and spiritual. The Bible is clear that sin does involve death as a consequence for disobedience (Gen. 2:17, Rom. 5:12ff) and the consequences of sin are understood in legal and punishment terms (note the judicial tones of 2 Thess. 1:6-9). But if the shedding of Christ's blood is divorced from the penalty of death for sin, then serious consequences readily follow.

To begin with, if one accepts that sin does involve a penalty, then the obvious question is what happens to that penalty.

---

6   See p 71.

The classical Christian doctrine of penal substitution answers this question by saying that Christ in his merciful love bears the penalty as a substitute for his people.[7] Yet the Westcott account of 'life released' has no *necessary* connection with paying sin's penalty for the believer. Naturally, one asks how sin's penalty is paid for, and by whom. If one has a doctrine of sin deserving punishment (and this is the Bible's testimony), then principles of distributive justice (which Ezekiel 18:20 and similar passages endorse) require the sinner to pay the penalty him or herself. It is hard to reconcile this with Paul's description of the blood of Jesus' Cross achieving peace in earth and heaven (Col. 1:20).

Of course, in our time the idea of God punishing for sin has in any case become more and more unpopular. For those committed to the view that God does not punish for sin, the 'life released' thesis looks highly attractive, because it offers an alternative explanation of

---

7   J.I. Packer's definition of penal substitution remains invaluable: '...Jesus Christ our Lord, moved by a love that was determined to do everything necessary to save us, endured and exhausted the destructive divine judgement for which we were otherwise inescapably destined, and so won us forgiveness, adoption and glory.' *Celebrating the Saving Work of God* (Carlisle: Paternoster, 1998), p. 105.

a prominent strand of language which does not depend on legal notions of punishment and justice. Rather, instead of understandings of Christ's work which include forensic elements, this tends to encourage an understanding of Christ's work which leans towards the therapeutic: Christ brings remedy or healing to those in need of life.

This idea of a therapeutic element in redemption requires further comment. It is important to remember that there is indeed a therapeutic element in Jesus' redemptive work. He speaks of his work with sinners in therapeutic terms in, for example, Luke 5:31. He is the Physician of the Soul. This means that responsible and comprehensive accounts of redemption will include notions of sin as sickness and those afflicted with it as in some ways victims. Some of these ways of explaining sin are helpful, and we might particularly mention here the metaphor of sin as addiction,[8] which is a particular instance of sin considered as sickness needing cure.

However, the tendency of Westcott's 'life released' account is not simply to set one

---

8   See e.g. J. Keith Miller, *Sin: Overcoming the Ultimate Deadly Addiction* (Harper Collins, 1987) and P.T McCormick, *Sin as Addiction* (Paulist Press, 1989).

biblical picture alongside another to provide a fuller account of Jesus' work. The tendency rather is to put forward an *alternative* view which tends to *exclude* understandings which link 'blood' with death and the penalty for sin. Minimally, this attenuates forensic and justice dimensions from Jesus' work. Stibbs' lucid examination of the texts of the Bible is therefore of the greatest value. Furthermore, his re-statement of the meaning of 'blood' in terms which do respect the forensic dimensions is not insisting on a penal substitutionary view of the Cross to the exclusion of others. Instead, Stibbs is the one sensitive to the wider range and subtleties of the Bible's thought because he preserves different dimensions to the Cross and Jesus' work by protecting a dimension which the 'life released' tends to gloss over. This point has not always been appreciated in recent discussions about penal substitution.

There is also a significant pastoral danger in advocating a therapeutic view of Jesus' work to the *exclusion* of sin as something requiring judgement and punishment. The point has been forcibly made that modern Anglophone cultures emphasise the therapeutic and the notion of victimhood, the so-called 'triumph of the therapeutic'.[9] This tends to minimise or even eliminate the notion that sin brings guilt under law, and is an offence against God. The pastoral danger that emerges in this guilt-free Christianity is that it also undermines any place for repentance.

The loss of repentance is serious indeed. In the first place, the Book of Acts features repeated calls precisely to repentance, culminating in Paul's teaching in Acts 17:30 that all people everywhere must repent. But furthermore, evangelical repentance is not merely a confession of guilt, a confession of who we are; it is also, as John Calvin notes,[10] a call on the merciful God to have mercy according to his promises, and a confession of who he is. In refusing to recognise who we are as guilty, we also do not recognise something about God.[11] This is the pastoral casualty, an attenuated sense of guilt breeding an attenuated sense of God's mercy.

---

9 See e.g. P Rieff, *The Triumph of the Therapeutic: Uses of Faith after Freud* (*Background: Essential Texts for the Conservative Mind*) (1st ed., 1966, re-issued: Intercollegiate Studies Institute, 2006) and P.C. Vitz, *Psychology as Religion: The Cult of Self-Worship* (Grand Rapids: Eerdmans, 1995).

10 *Institutes* III.3.2

11 Calvin notes the intense connection between our understanding of ourselves and our understanding of God in *Institutes* I.1.

No wonder, then, that the contemporary Church struggles with questions of God's love for us, our love for him, and assurance: we have lost a full appreciation of the dimensions of God's mercy, because exclusively therapeutic views actually underplay the wonder of what God has done. And Jesus himself warns that those who are forgiven little, or perceive themselves to have been forgiven little, love little: Luke 7:47.

Intriguingly, this is not the only point in Westcott's theology where one wonders whether something of the full grandeur of the saving work of Christ has been lost.[12] The same commentary on 1 John where the 'life released' view is developed also contains Westcott's essay 'The Gospel of Creation' in which he sets out the idea that Jesus would have become incarnate without the Fall. This shifts the Incarnation from a work primarily of salvific intent: it is salvific, but that is not *primarily* what it is about. Insensibly, the view of the reader is taken away from Jesus and his Cross as the 'main thing'. This possibility was taken further by Charles Gore and his fellow

---

12 Although other aspects of his work as an exegete remain of enduring value, for example in his commentary on the Gospel of John.

liberal catholic essayists in the collection *Lux Mundi* (1889).

For Stibbs, though, the Cross remains central. He will not let us forget the magnitude of the guilt-cleansing benefits of Jesus' death for his people. It is precisely on the themes of the greatness of Jesus' offering and the greatness of our sin against him that Stibbs ends his essay.[13] On the one hand, Stibbs' essay is a theological jewel, with its close and lucid reading of biblical material. On the other hand, it is a pastoral masterpiece, because the reader loves Christ more at the end of it. I think that would greatly please Alan Stibbs, and it is why this 'old' essay is so worth reading.

Michael Ovey
Oak Hill College
Spring 2011

---

13 See p 69.

Introduction

The meaning of the word 'blood' in Scripture is obviously of great importance to all Christian students of the Bible because of its frequent use in connection with Christ Himself and with the Christian doctrine of salvation. First, it is essential to an understanding of the Old Testament sacrifices to appreciate the meaning of the blood ritual, and the whole significance attached to 'blood' and to what was done with it. Secondly, and still more, it is essential to understand rightly the use and meaning of the word 'blood' in the New Testament, if we are properly to grasp the doctrinal interpretation of the work of Christ which was adopted and preached by the apostles and evangelists in the first decades of the

Christian church. What we need ultimately to discover and to be sure of is the theological significance of the word 'blood' in its use in the New Testament with reference to the sacrifice of Christ.

This is the more important because in this connection the word is used so often. As Vincent Taylor has pointed out, the 'blood' of Christ is mentioned in the writings of the New Testament nearly three times as often as 'the cross' of Christ and five times as frequently as the 'death' of Christ.[1] The term 'blood' is, in fact, a chief method of reference to the sacrifice of Christ, particularly in contexts which define its efficacy. Some adequate interpretation of the meaning of the term 'blood' cannot therefore be avoided if we are to continue to hold fast to New Testament Christianity. For, as Nathaniel Micklem has written, 'Not only the older form of evangelism, but every type of Biblical Christianity speaks of our salvation "by the blood of Christ"'.[2]

---

1   See Vincent Taylor, *The Atonement in New Testament Teaching* (second edition, London, 1945), p. 177. The distribution is as follows: Matthew (1), Mark (1), John (4), Acts (1), Pauline epistles (8), Hebrews (6), 1 Peter (2), 1 John (3), Revelation (4).

2   Nathaniel Micklem, *The Doctrine of Our Redemption* (London, 1943), p. 27.

A prevalent view – open to question

Interpretation is the more urgent because, as Dr Micklem goes on immediately to say in the same context, 'The phrase [the blood of Christ] is a stumbling-block to many in these days'. And in the judgement of the present writer this urgency is greatly increased because the line of interpretation commonly followed by the majority of modern writers is itself open to question as not true to the actual scriptural evidence.

According to this prevalent interpretation the phrase 'the blood of Christ' – to put it very briefly – stands not for His death but rather for His life released through death, and thus set free to be used for new purposes and made available for man's appropriation, particularly, as some would say, in the eucharist. Both the way in which this view is expressed and its prevalence among recent writers can best be indicated by some actual quotations. First, Dr Micklem says, in the same context as before, speaking of the Old Testament animal sacrifices:

> The blood of the victim is the life that has passed through death. When, therefore, we say that we are saved 'by the blood of Christ', we are ascribing our salvation,

not to the death of Christ nor to some mysterious transaction on Calvary, but to the life of Christ, the life that has passed through death.[3]

Next, Vincent Taylor, in several places in his books, seeks to force upon his readers the acceptance of this view as alone adequate to explain the scriptural statements. Speaking of animal sacrifice he says:

> ... destruction [of the victim] is not the primary intention. The victim is slain in order that its life, in the form of blood, may be released, and its flesh burnt in order that it may be transformed or etherealized; and in both cases the aim is to make it possible for life to be presented as an offering to the Deity. More and more students of comparative religion, and of the Old Testament worship in particular, are insisting that the bestowal of life is the fundamental idea in sacrificial worship.[4]

In commenting on the teaching of St Paul and his use of the term 'blood' with reference to the death of Christ, Vincent Taylor writes, 'To explain the allusions to "blood"

---

3   Ibid., p. 27.

4   Vincent Taylor, *Jesus and His Sacrifice: A Study of the Passion-Sayings in the Gospels* (London, 1937), pp. 54-55.

as synonyms for "death" is mistaken.'[5] In commenting on the epistle to the Hebrews, Vincent Taylor speaks of the writer's 'use of the word "blood" in relation to Christ in a sense entirely transcending the suggestion of a violent death'[6] and he adds later, 'it will be found, I think, that when he uses the term "blood" his main emphasis is upon the idea of life freely surrendered, applied and dedicated to the recovery of men'.[7] Writing of the fourth evangelist, Vincent Taylor says, 'the phrase "my blood" (in John 6:53-56) suggests the opportunity of life open to the appropriation of the believer'; and in the same context he incidentally observes, 'this thought of life released to be received is itself the vital concept without which no sacrificial theory can ever be adequately presented'.[8] Finally, in seeking to summarize the teaching of the New Testament on the doctrine of the atonement, Vincent Taylor writes, 'The sacrificial category is peculiarly suitable for this doctrinal presentation [of the work of Christ] because, in the use of the

---

5   Taylor, *Atonement*, p. 63.

6   Ibid., p. 121.

7   Ibid., p. 123.

8   Ibid., p. 149.

term "blood" it suggests the thought of life, dedicated, offered, transformed, and open to our spiritual appropriation'.[9]

Similarly, C.H. Dodd writes, 'In speaking of the Sacrament of the Lord's Supper (1 Cor. 10:16), Paul can say, 'The cup of blessing which we bless, is that not participating in the blood of Christ?' – i.e. participating in His life as dedicated to God.'[10] And O.C. Quick, commenting on the teaching of St John, writes, 'Blood represents the human life of Christ suffering, dying and sacrificed upon earth, which also cleanses Christians by being communicated to them in the Eucharist'.[11] Further, Bishop Hicks, writing on the development of sacrifice, asserts,

> Thus sacrifices are, in the first place, acts of fellowship between the god and members of the clan; and, later, are used for covenants, to create a blood brotherhood. ... In every case the blood is life released in order to be communicated.[12]

---

9   Ibid., p. 198.

10 C.H. Dodd, *The Epistle of Paul to the Romans*, Moffatt New Testament Commentary (London, 1932), p. 56.

11 O.C. Quick, *The Gospel of the New World: A Study in the Christian Doctrine of Atonement* (London, 1944), p. 56.

12 F.C.N. Hicks, *The Fullness of Sacrifice: An Essay in Reconciliation* (London, 1930), p. 34.

If we go back a generation to writers of forty and fifty years ago we also find some prevalence of the same ideas. For instance, P.T. Forsyth wrote, speaking of animal sacrifice,

> The pleasing thing to God and the effective element in the matter is not death but life. The blood was shed with the direct object not of killing the animal, but of detaching and releasing the life, isolating it, as it were, from the material base of body and flesh, and presenting it in this refined state to God.[13]

And in their commentary on the epistle to the Romans, Sanday and Headlam said,

> The significance of the Sacrificial Bloodshedding was twofold. The blood was regarded by the Hebrew as essentially the seat of life (Gen. 9:4, Lev. 17:11, Deut. 12:23). Hence the death of the victim was not only a death but a setting free of life; the application of the blood was an application of life; and the offering of the blood to God was an offering of life. In this lay more especially the virtue of the sacrifice.[14]

---

13 P.T. Forsyth, *The Cruciality of the Cross* (London, 1909), p. 186.

14 William Sanday and Arthur C. Headlam, *A Critical and Exegetical Commentary on the Epistle of the Romans* (fifth edition, Edinburgh, 1902), p. 89.

It is also significant that in this context, and again later, Sanday and Headlam explicitly confessed their authority for such a line of interpretation. They wrote,

> The idea of Vicarious Suffering is not the whole and not perhaps the culminating point in the conception of Sacrifice, for Dr Westcott seems to have sufficiently shown that the centre of the symbolism of Sacrifice lies not in the death of the victim but in the offering of its life.[15]

This is an important confession. For it seems clear enough that it is Bishop Westcott who is chiefly responsible for the widespread modern prevalence of this idea. In his commentary on the epistles of St John, first published in 1883, there is an additional note on 1 John 1:7 entitled *The Idea of Christ's Blood in the New Testament*. It seems desirable to quote a selection of his statements to indicate his teaching. With reference to the Old Testament sacrificial system he observes,

> By the outpouring of the Blood the life which was in it was not destroyed, though it was separated from the organism which it had before quickened. ... Thus two distinct

---

15   Ibid., p. 93.

ideas were included in the sacrifice of a victim, the death of the victim by the shedding of its blood, and the liberation, so to speak, of the principle of life by which it had been animated, so that this life became available for another end.[16]

After further discussion he adds,

Thus, in accordance with the typical teaching of the Levitical ordinances the Blood of Christ represents Christ's Life (1) as rendered in free self-sacrifice to God for men, and (2) as brought into perfect fellowship with God, having been set free by death. The Blood of Christ is, as shed, the Life of Christ given for men, and, as offered, the Life of Christ now given to men, the Life which is the spring of their life (John 12:24). ... The Blood always includes the thought of the life preserved and active beyond death.[17]

This conception of the Blood of Christ is fully brought out in the fundamental passage, John 6:53-56. Participation in Christ's Blood is participation in His life (v. 56). But at the same time it is implied throughout that it is only through His Death – His

---

16 B.F. Westcott, *The Epistles of St John: The Greek Text* (London, 1883), pp. 34-35.

17 Ibid., p. 35.

violent Death – that His Blood can be made available for men.[18]

It is no light task to set oneself against all this weight of scholarship. Yet it is the contention of the present writer that this view, thus eminently supported, is nevertheless open to question. And he is encouraged by the knowledge that in contending for a different interpretation he does not stand alone, nor is he advancing something new. Others have stood, and still stand, for the same interpretation as his. To mention three such writers. First, J. Armitage Robinson in his commentary on the epistle to the Ephesians, first published in 1903, says simply,

> To the Jewish mind 'blood' was not merely – nor even chiefly – the life-current flowing in the veins of the living: it was especially the life poured out in death; and yet more particularly in its religious aspect it was the symbol of sacrificial death.[19]

Second, Kittel's *Theological Dictionary* is the most recent attempt to define the scriptural

---

18 Ibid., p. 35. It is interesting and worthy of note that Bishop Westcott, in a footnote, virtually confesses his own indebtedness for some of his ideas to what he calls 'the very suggestive note' of William Milligan, *The Resurrection of Our Lord* (London, 1881), pp. 263-91.

19 J. Armitage Robinson, *St Paul's Epistle to the Ephesians* (London, 1903), p. 29.

and theological meaning of Greek New Testament words. In the article by Johannes Behm on the word αἷμα there is no reference whatever to the idea of life released. Behm gives a straightforward interpretation of the evidence of the New Testament usage itself and declares that 'blood', in the connection in which we are most interested in its use, stands for 'death'. Writers who speak of 'the blood of Christ' are interested not in the material substance but in the shed blood, that is, in the death of Christ. For the shedding of blood involves the destruction of the seat of life. And so the phrase 'the blood of Christ' is 'only a more vivid expression for the death of Christ in its redemptive significance'.[20]

Third, James Denney is particularly worth quoting because, in a book first published in 1902, he shows an awareness of Westcott's interpretation and an outspoken refusal to be fascinated by it. He says,

> It is by no means necessary, for the understanding of the evangelist [John] here, that we should adopt the strange caprice which fascinated Westcott, and

---

20 See Gerhard Kittel (ed.), *Theologisches Wörterbuch zum Neuen Testament* (10 vols, Stuttgart, 1932-78), vol. 1, pp. 171-5, article on αἷμα by Johannes Behm. See also Taylor, Atonement, p. 24.

distinguish with him in the blood of Christ (1) His death, and (2) His life; or (1) His blood shed, and (2) His blood offered; or (1) His life laid down, and (2) His life liberated and made available for men. No doubt these distinctions were meant to safeguard a real religious interest; they were meant to secure the truth that it is a living Saviour who saves, and that He actually does save, from sin, and that He does so in the last resort by the communication of His own life; but I venture to say that a more groundless fancy never haunted and troubled the interpretation of any part of Scripture than that which is introduced by this distinction into the Epistle to the Hebrews and the First Epistle of John. ... He [Christ] did something when He died, and that something He continues to make effective for men in His Risen Life; but there is no meaning in saying that by His death His life – as something other than His death – is 'liberated' and 'made available' for men.[21]

Such quotations are enough to indicate the issue which we have to face, and to anticipate the conclusion that we hope to justify. So bringing our introduction to a close, we must

---

21 James Denney, *The Death of Christ: Its Place and Interpretation in the New Testament* (revised edition, London, 1911), pp. 196-7.

now get to grips with a detailed examination and considered evaluation of the actual scriptural evidence.

1

Examination of Scriptural Usage in the Old Testament

General

The Hebrew word for 'blood', as the name for the red or purple fluid which circulates in men's arteries and veins, also had in the common speech of the people of Old Testament times a further significance which is readily understandable. When Joseph's brethren sold him to the merchantmen who were going to Egypt, they took Joseph's coat and dipped it in blood and sent it to Jacob. The sight of the blood made Jacob say, 'An evil beast hath devoured him' (Gen. 37:31-33). So blood directly suggested death, particularly a violent death. For when blood becomes visible and begins to flow, it means that damage has been done to someone's life; and when the blood is poured out in quantity and, so to speak, thought of in isolation as now separated from the body in which it flowed, it means that a life has been taken. So 'blood' became a word-symbol for 'death'. When the psalmist says, 'What profit is there in my blood?', he means, 'What profit is there in my death?' (Ps. 30:9).

Also, after a life has been taken by someone else, it is signs of the blood that may reveal the murderer. Someone with blood visibly upon him is immediately open to suspicion. And details of this kind, doubtless originally true in actual concrete cases, passed as pictures and thought-forms into the speech of the people and produced many vivid metaphorical phrases. A murderer was said to have upon him the blood of the person he had killed. Also, since murder demanded punishment or provoked revenge, the man who retaliated or inflicted the penalty was said to be avenging the murdered man's blood (see Num. 35:19, 26-27, Ps. 79:10). Such action was said to take the blood away from those responsible to take vengeance and to return it upon the head of the murderer (1 Kings 2:29-34). So in Proverbs we read of

'A man that is laden with the blood of any person' (Prov. 28:17 RV). Jonathan declared to Saul that to slay David without a cause would be to sin against innocent blood (1 Sam. 19:5). Jeremiah said, 'If ye put me to death, ye shall bring innocent blood upon yourselves, and upon this city, and upon the inhabitants thereof' (Jer. 26:15 RV). Further, if a person deserved to be put to death, or if his death was the result of his own folly, his blood was said to be on his own head and not on someone else's (Josh. 2:19, 2 Sam. 1:16, 1 Kings 2:37).

What is more, such metaphorical use of vivid word pictures involving 'blood' was apparently often resorted to, and sometimes in a surprisingly dramatic form, especially to indicate people's connection with someone's death. Judah said to his brethren about Joseph, 'What profit is it if we slay our brother, and conceal his blood?' (Gen. 37:26). Joab who 'shed the blood of war in peace' is said to have 'put the blood of war upon his girdle ... and in his shoes' (1 Kings 2:5, compare Jer. 2:34). When the righteous are to rejoice at the sight of vengeance on the wicked, the psalmist says they will wash their feet in the blood of the wicked (Ps. 58:10). To drink someone's blood (or to eat up his flesh, Ps. 27:2) meant not only to take his life, but to gain some advantage as a result of his death or at the price of taking away his life. So David, even when his three mighty men had done no more than put their lives in peril to fetch him water from the well of Bethlehem, said, 'Shall I drink the blood of these men that have put their lives in jeopardy?' (1 Chron. 11:17-19, 2 Sam. 23:15-17). Surely such metaphorical phraseology, and not least the fact that it is only metaphorical, must be of some significance to the Bible student in interpreting such New Testament statements as 'They washed their robes, and made them white in the blood of the Lamb' (Rev. 7:14), or 'He that eateth my flesh and drinketh my blood hath eternal life' (John 6:54 RV). Already we seem to see that in such phraseology 'blood' is a vivid word-symbol for referring to someone's violent death and for connecting other people with the consequences resulting from it.

Special: the language of religion
The significance of the word 'blood' in the Old Testament becomes even more

interesting and important once we recognize the inevitable Godward reference of the thought of all its writers; and still more when we consider the solemn ceremonies of religious worship. For it was what was done with 'blood' in the first Passover and in the regular sacrificial ritual, in putting it on places, things and people together with the recognition that nothing else but 'blood' would avail, which must have most influenced the development of the metaphorical phraseology of the everyday speech of the people, of which we have just instanced some examples.

In three places in the Old Testament the truth is dogmatically stated that the blood is the life (Gen. 9:4, Lev. 17:11, Deut. 12:23). This statement is emphatically quoted by those who assert that 'blood' stands for 'life' not 'death', because it seems at first sight to endorse that interpretation. But a careful examination of the contexts reveals that in each of the three cases these statements say not that 'blood' is 'life' in isolation, but that the blood is the life of the flesh. This means that if the blood is separated from the flesh, whether in man or beast, the present physical life in the flesh will come to an end. Blood shed stands, therefore, not for the release of life from the burden of the flesh, but for the bringing to an end of life in the flesh. It is a witness to physical death not an evidence of spiritual survival.

Further, the conviction that underlies the Old Testament Scriptures is that physical life is God's creation. So it belongs to Him and not to men. Also, particularly in the case of man made in God's image, this life is precious in God's sight. Therefore, not only has no man any independent right of freedom to shed blood and take life, but also, if he does, he will be accountable to God for his action. God will require blood of any man that sheds it. The murderer brings blood upon himself not only in the eyes of men but first of all in the sight of God. And the penalty which was due to God and which other men were made responsible to inflict, was that the murderer's own life must be taken. Such a man is not worthy to enjoy further the stewardship of the divine gift of life. He must pay the extreme earthly penalty and lose his own life in the flesh.

Further, the character of the punishment is also significantly described by the use of the word 'blood'. 'Whoso sheddeth man's blood, by man shall his blood be shed' (Gen. 9:5-6).

Again, human blood thus wrongly shed is said to pollute the land (Num. 35:33, Ps. 106:38). It is witness of a wrong done which must be visited upon the wrongdoer. Only so can innocent blood be put away from Israel (Deut. 19:11-13). It needs expiation, 'and no expiation can be made for the land for the blood that is shed therein, but by the blood of him that shed it' (Num. 35:33 RV). Also, until something is done to avenge such blood and to vindicate justice in God's sight, such blood can be said to cry out to God from the ground for something to be done (Gen. 4:10). It has, so to speak, the power to shout to heaven. For the taking of physical life is in God's sight so serious that it cannot rightly be overlooked. It raises an issue that demands settlement.

It is here in this realm of thought in which the right of shed blood to demand recompense is recognized, that Bishop Westcott in his

influential additional note begins to go wrong.[1]
For he misunderstands the vivid metaphorical
phraseology and suggests that statements that
blood already shed can cry to God are witness
that the blood is still alive after death. This surely
is a serious misunderstanding of metaphorical
language and a completely unjustified attempt
to suggest a very far-reaching conclusion on
wholly inadequate grounds. How can 'life' in
the full personal, rational and responsible sense
be attributed to blood, which has no power of

---

1   Westcott, *Epistles of John*, pp. 34-7. Since (as previously indicated)
Westcott acknowledges the suggestive character of a note by
Dr Milligan, it is perhaps worthy of note that Milligan makes
this very suggestion that shed blood is alive because of the way in
which it 'cries' to God. He says of the blood shed in sacrifice, 'No
reflecting person can imagine for a moment that blood, simply
as blood, could be acceptable to God. What made the blood
acceptable was that, as it flowed, it 'cried', confessing sin and
desert of punishment. It thus could not be dead. It was alive.
Not indeed that it was physically alive. It was rather ideally
alive – alive with a life which now assumed its true attitude
towards God, with a life which confessed, as it flowed forth in
the blood, that it was surrendered freely and in harmony with
the demands of God's righteous law. We know that the idea
of the blood thus speaking was familiar to the Jew (Gen. 4:10,
Job 16:18, Ezek. 24:7-8, Heb. 12:24), but what speaks either
must be, or must be thought of as being, alive. ... The blood
is a conventional hieroglyphic labelled as the life' (Milligan,
Resurrection, pp. 277-8). Here there seems to be obvious confusion
between the vivid meaning or significance attributed to shed
blood by men, and the actual persistence in the shed blood of the
living power to act or 'cry' on its own. The shed blood was not
still alive, but to intelligent and morally responsible men it did
visibly 'speak' of a life either violently taken or freely offered.

independent personal action? True, according to Scripture the 'blood' of a man after he is dead may cause things to happen. But that is not because the blood itself is still alive. The compelling cause is not the literal blood, not some persistent activity of the life that was in the blood, but the fact of the death or the life taken which the blood represents in the sight both of God and of men.

Next, there is in the Old Testament explicit indication that not only human life but animal life was equally recognized as God's. It could, therefore, only be taken by divine permission; and when it was taken God's ownership of the life that was taken had to be solemnly acknowledged. So, before their flesh could be rightly eaten, animals had to be slain before the Lord as unto Him; and their blood, which represented the life that had been taken, had to be either poured out on an altar or poured out to God on the ground and reverently covered. Any drinking of the blood was strictly forbidden (Gen. 9:4, Lev. 17:3-7, 10-14, Deut. 12:15-16, 20-28, 1 Sam. 14:32-35).

Such convictions and precepts gave all eating of animal flesh a religious significance, because the taking of the animal's life was something that had to be done unto God, as a 'sacrifice' unto Him and not just a slaying for men. Eating animal flesh, therefore, assumed the character of a sacrificial feast.[2] It was a meal only possible because God, to whom the life belonged, had allowed the life to be taken. It was a meal only possible by God's gift to men of part of the slain animal – that is, the flesh, which also was His. Such eating, therefore, was an occasion for thanksgiving to God. Such eating, too, was only possible at the cost of the animal's death. It was not a feeding upon the animal's life, but a feeding made possible by the animal's life being taken. The meal was a consequence of the animal's death. And the blood, which is the life of the flesh, was not released for men to partake. Rather, as a witness of animal life brought to an end, it was something too precious and too sacred to God for men to appropriate. So it had to be poured out unto God. A similar attitude not only to drinking blood as divinely forbidden, but also to the solemn significance of enjoying a benefit procured at the cost of the sacrifice of life, in this case human life, is

---

2   Compare the idea, prevalent in idolatry and witnessed to in 1 Corinthians 8-10, that meat was commonly not available to be eaten by men until it (as part of the animal slain to get it) had been offered to the idols first.

expressed in David's unwillingness to drink water procured at the risk of men's lives. He said, 'My God forbid it me, that I should do this: shall I drink the blood of these men that have put their lives in jeopardy?' And he did with the water what he would have done with blood. He poured it out unto the Lord (1 Chron. 11:17-19 RV).

What may now be seen in all its outstanding significance is the remarkable fact that the shed blood of animals, which it was otherwise forbidden to men to drink or in any way to use as theirs, was, so we read, given by divine appointment to be used to make atonement for sin and to effect expiation and cleansing (Lev. 17:11). Such were the virtue and value of a life laid down, particularly as a ransom for a life otherwise forfeit. Here instead of expiation by the blood of the guilty there was expiation by the blood of a guiltless substitute, a lamb without blemish and without spot.

The first and decisive example of this principle explicitly given in Scripture is in connection with the institution of the Passover (Exod. 12, compare Heb. 11:28). Here the blood of a lamb slain was appointed to be used by the Israelites to sprinkle on their doorposts to provide shelter and protection from divine judgement. The animal life thus to be taken had to be without blemish and, so to speak, not itself liable to death. Only so could its life be sacrificed as a substitute for another life under judgement that otherwise ought to have been taken. Once this spotless life was brought to an end and its blood shed, the value of the sacrifice was capable of being extended to shelter those in danger. This extension of the virtue and saving power of the animal's death was expressed by the sprinkling of the blood on the doorpost. The blood was not a 'release of life' for either God or men to partake. It is expressly said to be 'a token', which God would 'see' (Exod. 12:13). What mattered was its significance. And as a token it was a visible sign of life already taken. Those within the house who sheltered from judgement beneath the blood of the lamb, and feasted on its flesh, were not partakers in the animal's released life, but people enjoying the benefits of the animal's death. Also, such a provision by God of life given in sacrifice to ransom those whose lives were otherwise forfeit, purchased the beneficiaries. They were redeemed by blood; and redeemed not only from judgement but to be a people for the Lord's own possession.

There is a further application of this same principle in the ceremonial law and the sacrificial system of the Old Testament. Here we learn that the blood of animals, which man may not drink nor use for himself, has been given by God to men upon the altar to make atonement for their souls (Lev. 17:11). Such animal blood may, therefore, not only be shed and poured out to God as His upon the altar; it is also there to be regarded as given by divine appointment to cover sin; and it may, therefore, actually be appropriated for use and sprinkled upon things and people to secure ceremonial purification (see Exod. 29:1, 10-12, 15-16, 19-21, Lev. 3:2, 8, 13, 4:4-7, 15-18, 22-25, 16:14-19 etc.). Such action was not the completion of the making of the sacrifice, but the application of the virtue and the appropriation of the benefits of the sacrifice. Such blood could, so to speak, give access to God's presence. It could purify from defilement, at least symbolically, the holy place, the altar and the worshippers. For it was a witness to, or a token of, a spotless life sacrificed, which was more than a sufficient compensation in God's sight for the death due to the sinner, and which ultimately symbolized the spirit of utter obedience unto death and complete devotion to God which were all well-pleasing to Him. Such blood, therefore, far from crying out for investigation and vengeance cried out rather for acknowledgement and reward. It spoke better things than the blood of the murdered Abel. And just as the blood of someone wrongly slain could be on a person for condemnation, involving him in inevitable penalty, so this blood could be on a person or between him and God for expiation and cleansing, securing both his ransom and release from sin's penalty and his acceptance with God. It made him, ceremonially at least, fit for God's presence. Also, such benefits were all made available not through the release of the animal's life and participation in it, but through the applied virtue and value of the animal's life freely poured out in death in devotion to God, of which the animal's blood and what was done with it were adequate and intelligible symbols.

Before we close our survey of the Old Testament evidence, mention ought also to be made of the use of blood in covenant making, particularly at Sinai in the covenant between Jehovah and Israel when Moses took blood and sprinkled both the altar and the people and said, 'Behold the blood of the covenant which the Lord hath made with you' (Exod. 24:4-8). Here, as with the custom of passing between the divided pieces of slain animals in covenant making (see Gen. 15:7-21, Jer. 34:18-19), the intention of the symbolism seems clearly to have been to introduce in figure, and for purposes of solemn pledge, the death of the covenant maker. So the blood, particularly as sprinkled on the people, was a sign of death and not a vehicle for the communication of life.

To sum up thus far, the general witness of the Old Testament is, therefore, that 'blood' stands not for life released, but first for the fact and then for the significance of life laid down or taken in death.

2

2

Examination of Scriptural Usage in the New Testament

General

In the New Testament the word 'blood' (Greek αἷμα), while it is sometimes used in its direct literal sense to describe actual blood, is much more often used, as in the Old Testament, in a metaphorical sense as a way of referring to violent death and of connecting other people with it.

The word 'blood' first suggests the kind of damage to human life which threatens and results in death. So to 'resist unto blood' (Heb. 12:4) means to resist unto death, to die rather than yield. And when 'the souls of them that had been slain for the word of God, and for the testimony which they held' are said to cry, 'How long, O Master, the holy and true, dost thou not judge and avenge our blood?' (Rev. 6:10 RV), they obviously mean by avenge 'our blood' avenge 'our death', or rather the causing of our death and the shedding of our blood; or, as we might say, 'our murder'.

Similarly, to do something to endanger and to bring to an end someone's life is to have dealings with his blood. So after Judas had handed our Lord over to the chief priests, he confessed, 'I betrayed innocent blood'; and the money which he got for doing it was described by the chief priests as 'the price of blood' (Matt. 27:3-8 RV). Later Pilate, in his unwillingness to be responsible for giving sentence for Christ's crucifixion, said, 'I am innocent of the blood of this righteous man: see ye to it'. And all the people answered and said, 'His blood be on us, and on our children' (Matt. 27:24-25 RV). Again, after Pentecost the high priest said to Peter and the other apostles, 'Ye intend to bring this man's blood upon us' (Acts 5:28). This obviously means, 'You intend to hold us responsible and punishable for His death'. There is still more vivid language in the Apocalypse where Babylon is said to be a woman 'drunken with the blood of the saints, and ... martyrs of Jesus'. 'And in her was found the blood of prophets and of saints, and of all that have been slain upon the earth' (Rev. 17:6, 18:24 RV). Such phraseology is obviously metaphorical. It connects people with responsibility for someone's death. What really rests upon them is not actual blood, nor some virtue or vengeance of 'life released', but the defilement and guilt of blood shed, that is, of murder.

Blood thus shed by men may also be required of them, or come upon them, in judgement. So our Lord said that there shall 'come upon this generation' 'all the righteous blood shed on the earth, from the blood of Abel the righteous unto the blood of Zachariah son of Barachiah' (Matt. 23:34-36, Luke 11:50-51). In this statement it is significant that there occur the phrases 'the blood of Abel' and 'the blood of Zachariah', because they are phrases directly parallel in form to the phrase 'the blood of Christ'; and here the 'blood' of these men 'coming upon' the Jews of our Lord's day means, not the conveyance to the Jews of the released life of Abel and Zachariah, but the imposing on them of the consequences of their violent deaths.

We read, also, that on one occasion our Lord said to the scribes and Pharisees, 'Woe unto you', because they said, 'If we had been in the days of our fathers, we should not have been *partakers with them in the blood of the prophets*' (Matt. 23:29-30).[1] This description of men as 'partakers in the blood of' others is worthy of the more particular attention because of the somewhat parallel phraseology in 1 Corinthians, where Paul writes, 'The cup of blessing which we bless, is it not *a communion of the blood of Christ?*' (1 Cor. 10:16).[2] Clearly the phraseology used by our Lord describes men as sharers in the guilt of slaying the prophets, sharers, that is, in responsibility for their death and so men faced with the prospect of sharing in the punishment due in consequence of it. So we may in anticipation suggest that Paul meant of Christ that those who share in a communion in His blood are partakers, not in His released life, but in the consequences of His death – and, in this case, in its benefits and not in liability to judgement as those responsible for causing it.

Special: the blood of Christ

In turning now to consider passages in the New Testament which refer to the blood of

---

1   The significant words are κοινωνοὶ αὐτῶν ἐν τῷ αἵματι τῶν προφητῶν.

2   Here the somewhat parallel phrase is κοινωνία τοῦ αἵματος τοῦ Χριστοῦ.

Christ, one or two general comments seem desirable first, in order to suggest the main line of interpretation. This will also afford, in passing, welcome opportunity to refer to occurrences in the New Testament of the word 'blood' in the phrase 'flesh and blood' (see Matt. 16:17, 1 Cor. 15:50, Gal. 1:16, Eph. 6:12, Heb. 2:14). This phrase 'flesh and blood' stands for man's living body in its present earthly state. It indicates the condition and weakness of man's present physical nature as opposed to God and created spirits, and in contrast to the body that shall be in the resurrection. When the eternal Son of God became man He took a share in flesh and blood. So when the New Testament writers speak of 'the days of his flesh' (Heb. 5:7) or of knowing 'Christ after the flesh' (2 Cor. 5:16), the reference is to His earthly life – that is, the days of His flesh and blood, the days when, like other men, He had flesh kept alive by the blood that was in it. Similarly, when the New Testament writers speak of 'the blood of Christ' they are equally referring to His earthly life in the flesh and particularly to its violent end, that is, to what Paul specifically calls 'the blood of his cross' (Col. 1:20). Indeed, it is the more certain that the term 'the blood of Christ' can only refer to His earthly death. For, although our Lord spoke of His glorified body as having flesh and bones (Luke 24:39), there is no indication that it had any blood. Nor, indeed, is it likely; for the corruptible had put on incorruption (see and note 1 Cor. 15:50-53).

Also, there is in heaven no blood ritual such as there was in the Levitical tabernacle. For in the fulfilment of these divinely-ordained 'figures of the true', Christ Himself does not do things after His sacrifice with His blood, as something material and outside Himself which He comes before God to minister. He entered it not with, but 'through his own blood', that is, by means of or because of His death as Man when His human blood was shed (see Heb. 9:7, 11-12, 24-26). So in the heavenly glory He does not sprinkle and never has actually sprinkled blood upon some heavenly mercy-seat.[3] Rather He is Himself, so to speak, the mercy-seat or propitiation, being Himself already sufficiently 'blood-stained' by reason of His death on the cross. He partook of flesh and blood to 'taste death for every man' and 'that through death he might bring to nought him that had the power of death,

---

3   Some fuller exposition of this point follows below.

that is, the devil'; and it is 'because of the suffering of death' that we now behold Jesus 'crowned with glory and honour' and able as the pioneer of man's salvation to bring His many brethren as sons of God into the same glory (see Heb. 2:5-17). He is for ever accepted and enthroned, worshipped and honoured, and assured of final and complete triumph, because He is the 'Lamb as it had been slain' (see Rev. 5:6). So the term 'the blood of Christ' is a metaphorical or symbolical way of referring to His earthly death in a human body upon a cross of shame, and to its innumerable and eternal consequences. And it is these benefits of His passion that are meant to be conveyed to and enjoyed by all who are said either to be sprinkled by His blood or to drink symbolically of it.

We now pass to a more detailed examination of passages in the New Testament in which explicit reference is made to the blood of Christ, together with a few closely allied passages in the epistle to the Hebrews which refer to the ceremonial uses of blood under the old covenant.

a) Romans 3:25 RV: 'Whom God set forth to be a propitiation, through faith, by his blood' (ὃν προέθετο ὁ Θεὸς ἱλαστήριον διὰ τῆς πίστεως ἐν τῷ αὐτοῦ αἵματι).

Here προέθετο may convey the sense of 'set forth openly' or 'made a public spectacle', in contrast to the Levitical sprinkling of the mercy-seat which was hidden from the sight of the people. In that case it means that on the cross, Jesus was openly displayed as propitiatory in the suffering of death or by the shedding of His blood. Some would, of course, translate ιλαστήριον as 'mercy-seat' and thus make Christ the mercy-seat. Sanday and Headlam say, 'There is great harshness, not to say confusion, in making Christ at once priest and victim and place of sprinkling'. And they add, 'The Christian ιλαστήριον or "place of sprinkling", in the literal sense, is rather the Cross'.[4] This thought corresponds, too, to the foregoing interpretation of the verse, an interpretation which focuses all attention on Christ's death, on the shedding of His blood on the cross. If, however, προέθετο means 'purposed' or 'foreordained' and we do translate, 'whom God foreordained to be the mercy-seat – in His blood', the suggestion then is not that after His death Christ sprinkled blood on some heavenly mercy-seat, but that He

---

4   Sanday and Headlam, *Romans*, p. 87.

Himself is the true, eternal mercy-seat of the divine purpose 'by his blood', that is, because of His death as Man for men. This corresponds to the statement in 1 John that, in the presence of God, Christ Himself, and not some further sprinkling of His blood, is the propitiation for our sins (1 John 2:1-2). Also, whichever interpretation we prefer, the phrase 'in his blood' refers equally to the event of His death as Man on the cross.

b) Romans 5:9 RV: 'Much more then, being now justified by his blood (δικαιωθέντες νῦν ἐν τῷ αἵματι αὐτοῦ), shall we be saved from the wrath [of God] through him.'

In this context the three previous verses all refer exclusively to dying and emphatically to Christ's death for us sinners. The sequence of thought demands, therefore, that the words 'his blood' must refer to His dying for us. Also, while in this verse and the next there are double references to complementary aspects of full salvation, the parallelism demands that 'being justified by his blood' in verse 9 should be regarded as more or less equal to 'while we were enemies, we were reconciled to God through the death of his Son' in verse 10; and not with the idea that we shall be 'saved by his life'. In other words, justification is a benefit made ours through His death for us. Again to quote Sanday and Headlam, 'He [Paul] … clearly connects the act of justification with the bloodshedding of Christ'.[5]

c) Ephesians 1:7 RV: 'In whom we have redemption through his blood (διὰ τοῦ αἵματος αὐτου), the forgiveness of our trespasses.'

1 Peter 1:18-19 RV: 'Knowing that ye were redeemed … with precious blood (τιμίῳ αἵματι), as of a lamb without blemish and without spot.'

Acts 20:28 RV: 'The church of God, which he purchased with his own blood' (ἣν περιεποιήσατο διὰ τοῦ αἵματος τοῦ ἰδίου).

Revelation 5:9 RV: 'For thou wast slain, and didst purchase unto God with thy blood (ἐν τῷ αἵματί σου) men of every tribe, and tongue, and people, and nation.'

In these passages the reference is to 'blood' as the 'ransom' or 'purchase price'. Commenting on 'through his blood' in Ephesians 1:7, Bishop Lightfoot wrote, 'This is the ransom-money, the λύτρον (Matt. 20:28; Mark 10:45), or

---

ἀντίλυτρον (1 Tim. 2:6, compare Titus 2:14), the price, τιμη. (1 Cor. 6:20, 7:23), for which we were bought.'[6] Such a ransom was under the law some equivalent compensation and in this case obviously 'life' for 'life' or 'blood' for 'blood'. Since the sinner's life was forfeit and subject to death, Christ could only redeem the sinner and break the hold of sin and give release (what Paul calls τὴν ἄφεσιν τῶν παραπτωμάτων, Eph. 1:7) by His blood; that is, by Himself as Man suffering death in the sinner's stead. This act also purchased the redeemed as His own property. The church is His because He laid down His life for it. As Paul indicates in Titus 2:14, Christ secured both our redemption from iniquity and the rights of possession over us by giving Himself for us. 'His blood' therefore – described possibly in Acts 20:28 as 'the blood of God' or 'God's very own blood' – means the outpouring in death of that human life which He had made His own by becoming Man. It is a reference to His one act of final sacrifice on earth in the days of His flesh and blood, when He gave up His human body to be nailed to the tree.

---

6   J.B. Lightfoot, *Notes on Epistles of St Paul from Unpublished Commentaries* (London, 1895), p. 316.

d) Ephesians 2:13 RV: 'But now in Christ Jesus ye that once were far off are made nigh in the blood of Christ' (ἐν τῷ αἵματι τοῦ Χριστοῦ).

This verse comes in a paragraph which refers to the bringing in of the Gentiles, who had been complete outsiders, to become fellow-citizens with the saints and full members of the family or household of God. Hitherto, as the dividing wall of the Jewish Temple courts symbolized, they had been both shut out from nearer access to God and separated from full fellowship with Israel. Now they are reconciled both to God and to man; and, says Paul in the same context, Christ abolished the enmity 'in his flesh', or through His incarnation and earthly life; and He actually achieved the full victory and slew the enmity by means of the cross. It is, therefore, 'through the cross' that He reconciles them both unto God (see Eph 2:11-22, especially vv. 14-18). When, therefore, Paul said previously that those once afar off are made nigh 'in the blood of Christ' he unquestionably means, as he immediately explains, that they are made nigh as a consequence of Christ's death upon the cross.

e) Colossians 1:19-20 RV: 'For it was the good pleasure [of the Father] that in him should all the fulness dwell; and through him to reconcile all things unto himself, having made peace through the blood of his cross' (ἐιρηνοποιήσας διὰ τοῦ αἵματος τοῦ σταυροῦ αὐτου).

Again, the thought is of reconciliation of all things to God, and of doing away with the enmity and estrangement caused by sin. It is those who in times past were alienated and enemies in their mind in their evil works that Christ has now reconciled to present them holy and without blemish and unreprovable before Him (see Col. 1:19-22). How then has He done this? Paul says first not only 'through his blood' but 'through the blood of his cross'; and he makes his meaning doubly and unmistakably plain by adding 'in the body of his flesh through death'. There were in Colossae Gnostic tendencies to despise things earthly, fleshly and material, and to believe that the holy things of God, and much more His personal appearing and activity, could not be fully of or in this world. Paul's answer to such heresy was direct and emphatic. He declares that the universal reconciliation has been effected through something done in history, in a human body of flesh and on a cross of shame; and it was done through physical dying. So 'the blood of his cross' can mean no other than the pouring out in death of His earthly human life by crucifixion on a common gibbet. That is the deed that avails to put men right with God.

f) Hebrews 9:7 RV: 'but into the second went the high priest alone, once in the year, not without blood (οὐ χωρὶς αἵματος) which he offereth for himself, and for the errors of the people.'

Hebrews 9:11-14 RV: 'But Christ ... through his own blood (διὰ δὲ τοῦ ἰδίου αἵματος) entered in once for all into the holy place. ... For if the blood of goats and bulls, and the ashes of a heifer sprinkling them that have been defiled, sanctify unto the cleanness of the flesh: how much more shall the blood of Christ, who through the eternal Spirit offered himself without blemish unto God, cleanse your conscience from dead works to serve the living God?'

Hebrews 9:22: 'And, according to the law, I may almost say, all things are cleansed with blood (ἐν αἵματι), and apart from shedding of blood there is no remission' (καὶ χωρὶς αἱματεκχυσίας οὐ γίνεται ἄφεσις).

Hebrews 9:25 RV: 'as the high priest entereth into the holy place year by year with blood not his own' (ἐν αἵματι ἀλλοτρίῳ).

Hebrews 10:4 RV: 'It is impossible that the blood of bulls and goats should take away sins.'

Hebrews 10:19-20, 22 RV: 'Having therefore, brethren, boldness to enter into the holy place by the blood of Jesus (ἐν τῷ αἵματι Ἰησου), by the way which he dedicated for us, a new and living way, through the veil, that is to say, his flesh; ... let us draw near ... having our hearts sprinkled from an evil conscience.'

These verses deserve much more detailed attention than we can here give them. Further, in this paper their significance has already been partly anticipated. To comment briefly: the main objective of the priestly ministry was clearly to remove the barriers and estrangement caused by sin and to gain access to God's presence. Under the old order of the Jewish tabernacle the true way in was not yet made manifest (see Heb. 9:8). The high priest, who did enter once a year into the most holy place, could only do so 'not without blood' and 'with blood not his own'. This taking of blood into the holy place was a token of blood already shed and of a life laid down in expiation for sin. But Christ did not enter 'with blood' or taking blood at all. He entered *through his own blood*, that is, by way of His own death; in which way He did not cease to act when as Man He died, because as God He was also an eternal and undying Spirit. He could, as none else could, offer Himself in the act of dying. When His blood was shed He made a present immediate offering or sacrifice of Himself to God in 'the greater and more perfect tabernacle' (see Heb. 9:11-12, 23-26). His flesh (made sin for us) became as it were the separating veil and was rent; and as His blood flowed forth in death a new and living way to God was opened up and consecrated for us; as, also, in the very hour in which He yielded up His spirit, the veil of the symbolical temple was rent in twain from the top to the bottom (Mark 15:37-38). Thus He entered into the true immediate Presence of God 'through his blood', when He offered Himself to God on the cross; and He thus entered once for all, never again needing to offer anything further to secure entrance either for Himself as man's high priest or for His people.

For Christ's resurrection and ascension, which are significantly not mentioned in this whole context, were not stages in the sacrificial presentation of Himself or of His offering to God. Rather they were subsequent stages of triumph and exaltation for His humanity, consequent upon a work already finished and a victory won. It was the enthronement of the high priest whose work of making propitiation was already finished. Christ did not offer His glorified body to God, but the body of His flesh in death, the body of flesh and blood in which He bore our sin. And just as He entered into God's Presence 'through his blood', or by reason of His human death, so all His people are bidden to have boldness to enter into the holy place by the same blood of Jesus, appropriating for themselves the benefits of His death and walking in the way which, because of His dying for us, now stands open. 'By the blood of Jesus' means, therefore, through the death of Jesus and its realized significance.

Again, under the old Levitical order the blood of goats and bulls and the ashes of a heifer were sprinkled upon men to secure for them ceremonial purity. This reference to ashes of a burnt corpse suggests that what is being signified is not the released life of the victim but its accomplished death. It was this that had virtue to atone and to sanctify; and this virtue, be it noted, could continue to operate after and indeed because the animal's life had been taken. Participation in this virtue or benefit from the animal's sacrifice already accomplished, was symbolized by sprinkling men with its blood or with its ashes mixed with water. Similarly, and much more, Christ's one act as Man of offering Himself to God in death for sin has an abiding value and efficacy. It continually avails to secure not just ceremonial cleansing but inner moral purification and release from bondage. Its power thus to cleanse is inexhaustible and still available. This continuing efficacy of the one past act of sacrifice to give men present cleansing is expressed in language provided by the Old Testament by describing the cleansing as done by the blood of Christ. The cleansing is a present benefit which is made available and actual because of the one sufficient sacrifice made when the incarnate Son of God shed for men His human blood. So, as this writer to the Hebrews also says, it is by this one offering of His human body once for all that He has perfected for ever them that are sanctified (see Heb. 10:10-14).

g) Hebrews 12:24 RV: 'and to Jesus the mediator of a new covenant, and to the blood of sprinkling that speaketh better than that of Abel.'

1 Peter 1:2: 'unto obedience and sprinkling of the blood of Jesus Christ.'

1 John 1:7: 'and the blood of Jesus Christ his Son cleanseth us from all sin.'

These verses all pursue the thought just commented on above. Sacrifice of life is so significant in God's sight that the blood thus shed has, so to speak, power to cry out afterwards either for recompense or reward; and to secure a share in these consequences for those either involved in it or sprinkled by it.

> Abel's blood for vengeance
> Pleaded to the skies;
> But the blood of Jesus
> For our pardon cries.
> Oft as it is sprinkled

On our guilty hearts,
Satan in confusion
Terror-struck departs.

'The sprinkling of the blood' in the case of Christ's sacrifice means the extension to the persons sprinkled of the value and the benefits of the death of which it is the token.[7] So the phrase and the idea continue to be a metaphorical way of referring to the application of and the participation in the saving benefits of the death of Jesus.[8] This efficacy of the one sacrifice already made is continuous and all-sufficient. So Christians can still prove, as they walk in the light, that the blood of Jesus cleanses them from all sin; that is, that Christ's death avails to purge away any and every fresh defilement. Here, too, in 1 John it is significant that John, who is often so occupied in thought with the believer's

---

7   Compare: 'He [Paul] conceives of that Death as operating by a sacrificial blood-shedding. The Blood of that Sacrifice is as it were sprinkled round the Christian, and forms a sort of hallowed enclosure, a place of sanctuary, into which he enters. Within this he is safe, and from its shelter he looks out exultingly over the physical dangers which threaten him; they may strengthen his firmness of purpose but cannot shake it.' Sanday and Headlam, *Romans*, p. 119.

8   For its connection also with the new covenant note Heb. 12:24a, compare Exod. 24:7-8 and see the following section on covenant blood.

participation in Christ's life, attributes to the blood of Jesus not the power to quicken but the power to cleanse. For the quickening or regenerating work which gives men new life is done by the Spirit, not by the blood.[9]

h) Matthew 26:27-28 RV: 'And he took a cup, and gave thanks, and gave to them, saying Drink ye all of it, for this is my blood of the covenant, which is shed for many unto remission of sins.' (See also Mark 14:24, Luke 22:20, 1 Cor. 11:25-27.)

Hebrews 9:15-20 RV: 'And for this cause he is the mediator of a new covenant, that a death having taken place for the redemption of the transgressions that were under the first covenant, they that have been called may receive the promise of the eternal inheritance. For where a testament is, there must of necessity be the death of him that made it. For a testament is of force where there hath been death: for doth it ever avail while he that made

---

9   Compare John 6:52-63. It is noteworthy that when our Lord spoke of gaining life through eating His flesh and drinking His blood, He added, 'It is the spirit that quickeneth; the flesh profiteth nothing.' This seems to mean that there is no life actually transmitted through the material flesh and blood; but rather that, as a result of His atoning death and as a benefit of His passion, the Spirit is given to give men new life. Compare John 7:37-39.

it liveth? Wherefore even the first covenant hath not been dedicated without blood. For when every commandment had been spoken by Moses unto all the people according to the law, he took the blood of the calves and the goats, with water and scarlet wool and hyssop, and sprinkled both the book itself, and all the people, saying, This is the blood of the covenant which God commanded to you-ward.'

Hebrews 10:29: 'and hath counted the blood of the covenant, wherewith he was sanctified, an unholy thing.'

Hebrews 13:20-21: 'with [or 'by'] the blood of the eternal covenant' (ἐν αἵματι διαθήκης αἰωνίου).

There are more references to 'the blood of the covenant' than we can here examine in detail. Covenants seem clearly to have been dedicated with blood (note Heb. 9:18) as a symbolic representation of the death of the covenant-maker. In ordinary human transactions such symbolism was presumably a vivid witness before God to what the individuals concerned condemned themselves to suffer if they failed to fulfil their covenant undertakings. They swore by their lives; if they failed – let their blood be shed. But in the perfect eternal covenant in Christ's blood there is more than this. For the death that actually took place was the death of the incarnate Son of God. And so the blood with which this new covenant was dedicated affords 'cover' to give actual remission of sins. It can make men clean from all defilement. For, as the writer to the Hebrews says, 'a death' has 'taken place for the redemption of the transgressions that were under the first covenant' (Heb. 9:15 RV). So Christ is the mediator of a new covenant 'which hath been enacted upon better promises' (Heb. 8:6 RV) and by which, as did not prove true under the old covenant, reception of the promised inheritance by those called is absolutely sure. For in this new covenant, because of Christ's blood that was shed, there is a guarantee that those who share in it will not fail in the middle nor be found wanting at the last. The God of peace, who showed His acceptance of what Jesus had done for men by bringing Him as the great Shepherd of the sheep again from the dead, will for the same reason do more and do all. Because of Christ's accomplished sacrifice and by the blood of the eternal covenant thus sealed, God Himself can be counted on to make all the sheep for whom the Shepherd laid down His life perfect in every good thing to do His will (Heb. 13:20-21). Nor is any further offering of His sacrifice for their sins necessary, even though they commit fresh sins. For where remission of sins is – and that is what, according to Christ's own words, the blood of the covenant assures us of when we drink the cup[10] – there is no more offering for sin (Heb. 10:18).[11] So the cup of the covenant blood is not a means of participation in life released to be communicated, but a visible seal of eternal redemption fully obtained for us by Christ's death and now available to be enjoyed and offered for faith's appropriation.[12]

i) John 6:54-58 RV: 'He that eateth my flesh and drinketh my blood hath eternal life .... For my flesh is meat indeed, and my blood is drink indeed [or 'true drink']. He that eateth my flesh and drinketh my blood abideth in me and I in him.'

---

10 Note Matt. 26:28 rv, 'unto remission of sins'.

11 Alternatively, for those who deliberately reject this one sacrifice there is no other second sacrifice held in reserve; they have no prospect but judgement. See Heb. 10:26-31.

12 Of course, this redemption includes Christ's gift of life and life more abundant. The point here is that this new life is not directly signified by, released in, or communicated through 'the blood of Christ'.

Revelation 1:5 RV: 'Unto him that loveth us and loosed [or 'washed'] us from our sins by his blood' (ἐν τῷ αἵματι αὐτοῦ).

Revelation 7:14 RV: 'These are they which come out of great tribulation, and they washed their robes, and made them white in the blood of the Lamb' (ἐν τῷ αἵματι τοῦ ἀρνίου).

Revelation 12:11 RV: 'And they overcame him because of the blood of the Lamb' (διὰ τὸ αἷμα τοῦ ἀρνίου).

We have surely surveyed enough scriptural quotations already to see that for those who have entered into the heritage of Scripture there is every justification for the most vivid metaphorical use of the word 'blood' in phrases that express the benefits that become ours through Christ's death for us. Such metaphorical language is found nowhere more vividly applied than on the lips of Christ Himself. He spoke of the necessity of 'drinking his blood' and said, 'My blood is true drink'. And we venture to assert that our previous study has made it abundantly clear that such language describes not participation in His life but appropriation of the benefits of His life laid down. To eat His flesh and to drink

His blood is to confess that only through His death can I live. As the familiar Prayer Book language asserts, it is 'The blood of our Lord Jesus Christ which was shed for thee' (not 'which is now being given to thee') which can 'preserve thy body and soul unto everlasting life'.[13] We drink the cup in remembrance of the one act of sacrifice – His blood shed – and in appropriation of its benefits.

Similarly, in the Apocalypse there are vivid metaphorical phrases which are not an indication of some crude 'religion of the shambles', but a purely figurative method of rejoicing in salvation through Christ's death. So we give Him honour who has 'loosed [or 'washed'] us from our sins by his blood'. The multitude of the redeemed, who stand before God's throne, are they who 'washed their robes and made them white in the blood of the Lamb'. The Christian brethren overcome the devil who would accuse them before God, 'because of the blood of the Lamb'. Such language attributes freedom, cleansing and final triumph over all condemnation all to the virtue of Christ's one sacrifice for His people when, as Man, He shed His human blood.

---

13 Words used in the administration of the cup in the Holy Communion.

What the writers of the New Testament thus began, the Christian worshippers in song – the hymn-writers of the church – have ever since sustained. They still know, as some so-called theologians apparently do not know, how to glory in the blood of the Lamb and thus to sing the praise of Him who died. For Christ's death for us is 'the sinner's hope', the unending cause of all our blessings. It can, therefore, even in heaven itself, never cease to be the central theme of all the worship. 'Worthy is the Lamb that hath been slain to receive the power, and riches, and wisdom, and might, and honour, and glory, and blessing' (Rev. 5:12 RV). Let him who can, refrain from saying 'Amen'.

Conclusion

Some attempt must now be made to sum up our findings and to make some final comments. Before we do this, let us notice two general considerations essential to a right understanding of the meaning of the word 'blood' in the Bible. First, there is nothing in the ideas of the Bible about 'blood' which is at all comparable to the modern practice of blood transfusion. Nowadays one man can sometimes say of another, 'He gave his blood to me'. This is not a right thing for the Christian to say of Christ. To talk of 'the drinking of his blood' with reference to participation in the Holy Communion, or thus to describe the response of appropriating faith, is something entirely symbolical or metaphorical. And it is well for us to note that the Jewish abhorrence of all actual blood-drinking was recognized and respected in the early church (see Acts 15:28-29). Clearly, therefore, none thought that Christ had given them His actual blood to drink as the way of being renewed by His life.

Second, we are very prone to forget that the shedding of blood is in man's experience wholly a consequence of sin. Man was not originally intended by God to die in this way. Apart from sin, man would have entered into glory by translation and transfiguration, as is suggested in the cases of Enoch and Elijah (Gen. 5:24, 2 Kings 2:11) and made finally plain by our Lord's own transfiguration. As sinless Man, Jesus could have gone to heaven that way; but He chose to accomplish a different kind of 'exodus' in Jerusalem and to shed His blood as the Passover lamb for the redemption of His people (see Luke 9:28-36). To speak, therefore, of Christ's shed blood is to acknowledge the amazing fact that He, the sinless Son of God, actually as Man, died the kind of death which only sinners ought to die. All our references to 'Christ's blood' ought therefore to involve the significant recollection that His human life in this world came to an end by the violent rending of His flesh and that, as though He

Himself were a sinner, He died the sinner's kind of death (that is, a blood-shedding death); and it is because He died the kind of death that sinners ought to die, that sinners can by faith in Him and Him crucified be saved from sin and all its dire consequences.

For, 'being found in fashion as a man, he humbled himself, becoming obedient even unto death, yea, the death of the cross' (Phil. 2:8 RV). This is the amazing condescension to which the New Testament writers bear witness when they say that 'Christ died for us', and that we are 'justified by his blood'. This is equally the amazing condescension which still inspires the unceasing wonder and worship of His people. It is, therefore, when the redeemed sing the praise of the Lamb who died, that the word 'blood' is spontaneously given its true scriptural meaning. So, for example, it is that one has written,

> Bearing shame and scoffing rude,
> In my place condemned He stood;
> Sealed my pardon with His blood:
> Hallelujah! What a Saviour!

Now, let us seek to sum up more generally and more comprehensively the main significance of the word 'blood' as we have seen it to be used throughout the whole Bible. Blood is a visible token of life violently ended; it is a sign of life either given or taken in death. Such giving or taking of life is, in this world, the extreme, both of gift or price and of crime or penalty. Man knows no greater. So, first, the greatest offering or service one can render is to give one's blood or life. 'Greater love hath no man than this, that a man lay down his life for his friends' (John 15:13). Second, the greatest earthly crime or evil is to take blood or life, that is, manslaughter or murder. Third, the great penalty or loss is to have one's blood shed or life taken. So it says of the blood-shedder, 'by man shall his blood be shed'; and so Paul says of the magistrate, 'He bareth not the sword in vain: for he is a minister of God, an avenger for wrath to him that doeth evil' (Rom. 13:4 RV). 'The wages of sin is death' (Rom. 6:23). Fourth, the only possible or adequate expiation or atonement is life for life and blood for blood. This expiation man cannot give (see Ps. 49:7-8, Mark 8:36-37). Not only is his own life already forfeit as a sinner, but also all life is God's (see Ps. 50:9-10). So man has no 'blood' that he can give. This necessary but otherwise unobtainable gift God has given. He has given the blood to make atonement (Lev. 17:11). Atonement is, therefore, only possible by the gift of God. Or as P. T. Forsyth expressed it, sacrifice 'is the fruit of grace and not its root'.[1] What is more, when our Lord claimed to have come 'to give his life a ransom for many' (Mark 10:45), He was implying His deity as well as His human sinlessness and indicating the fulfilment of that which the shed blood of animal sacrifices merely typified. Here in Jesus, the incarnate Son, was God come in person to give, as Man, the blood which only can make atonement. The church of God is, therefore, purchased with His own blood (Acts 20:28).

All these four significances of 'blood' as shed meet in the cross of Christ. There the Son of Man in our flesh and blood for us men and for our salvation made the greatest offering. He gave His life (see John 10:17-18). Second, He became the victim of mankind's greatest crime. He was vilely and unjustly put to death. Third, 'He was reckoned with transgressors' (Luke 22:37 RV, from Isa. 53:12) and endured the extreme penalty

---

1   William Sanday (ed.), *Different Conceptions of Priesthood and Sacrifice: A Report of a Conference Held at Oxford* (London, 1900), p. 93. Compare, 'The atonement did not procure grace, it flowed from grace.' 'The positive truth is that the sacrifice is the result of God's grace and not its cause. It is given by God before it is given to Him.' Forsyth, *Cruciality of the Cross*, pp. 78, 185.

of the wrongdoer. The hand of the law and of the Roman magistrate put Him to death. By man was His blood shed. Fourth, He as God made flesh gave, as He alone could do, His human blood to make atonement. Repentance and remission of sins can, therefore, now be preached in His Name. We are justified by His blood.

So, 'the blood of Christ' speaks to us, as Archbishop Cranmer said of the bread and wine in the Lord's Supper, of Christ *ut in cruce non in caelo*. 'To drink his blood' means not to appropriate His life, nor to feed upon His glorified humanity, nor to draw upon the power of His resurrection – with the cross put into the background as but a necessary preliminary to release the life. Rather does it mean consciously, and by faith alone, humbly to appropriate all our blessings and not least redemption and cleansing from sin as wholly and solely the benefits of His death.

Further, this one act in history of the death of Jesus – the offering of His body and the shedding of His blood – is of such value that it avails to reconcile all things unto God and to perfect for ever those whom it sanctifies. Such is the value in eternity of the Lamb slain. This one offering has an all-sufficient efficacy to cover the sins passed over before Christ came, and to cleanse completely all those who are being brought in until the church is complete. The 'broken pieces' which (as in the feeding of the five thousand) are more than enough to satisfy the whole multitude, all come from His one breaking of the bread. So William Cowper was right and truly scriptural both in doctrine and in language when he taught us to sing:

> Dear dying Lamb, Thy precious blood
> Shall never lose its power,
> Till all the ransomed Church of God
> Is saved to sin no more.

In conclusion, therefore, we regretfully disagree with Bishop Westcott (to whose exposition of Scripture we owe so much) and with his many modern disciples, when they say that 'the blood of Christ' signifies His life released through death and thus made available for new uses; and we endorse as right the exegesis and the judgement of those who have said that the phrase 'the blood of Christ' is, like the word 'cross', 'only a more vivid expression for the death of Christ in its redemptive significance'.[2] 'It connotes the sacrificial death of Christ and all its remedial issues.'[3]

---

2   Johannes Behm in Kittel, *Theologisches Wörterbuch*.

3   W. Saumarez Smith quoted by Nathaniel Dimock, *The Doctrine of the Death of Christ* (second edition, London, 1903), p. 63.

About the Author

Alan Stibbs (1901-1971) was born into a Christian family and responded personally to the call of Christ in 1912. He began to give his first Bible exposition at 16 years old and was later called to the mission field. His preaching & teaching led him to the staff of Oakhill theological college and he became known as a Bible expositor and preacher in demand for evangelical conferences and conventions.

SUCH
A GREAT
SALVATION

The collected essays of
Alan Stibbs

edited by Andrew Atherstone

ISBN 978-1-84550-423-6

Such a Great Salvation

The Collected Essays of Alan Stibbs

EDITED BY ANDREW ATHERSTONE

Alan Stibbs was a voice crying in the wilderness, a lonely evangelical scholar in a sea of liberalism. We owe him much.

> John Stott
> Rector Emeritus,
> All Souls Church,
> Langham Place, London

In this volume, eighteen of Alan Stibbs' best and most enduring shorter writings are brought together. They cover themes such as the cross of Christ, justification by faith, the inspiration of Scripture, the priority of preaching, the nature of the church, and the role of the sacraments.

Andrew Atherstone is tutor in history and doctrine, and Latimer research fellow, at Wycliffe Hall, Oxford. His publications include *Oxford's Protestant Spy: The Controversial Career of Charles Golightly* (2007), *The Martyrs of Mary Tudor* (second edition, 2007) and *Oxford: City of Saints, Scholars and Dreaming Spires* (2008). He is also editor of *The Heart of Faith: Following Christ in the Church of England* (2008).

CROSS WORDS

THE BIBLICAL DOCTRINE OF THE ATONEMENT

PAUL WELLS

ISBN 978-1-84550-118-1

Cross Words

The Biblical Doctrine of the Atonement

PAUL WELLS

The post-modern society is so focussed on the internal life of the individual that it makes the significance of the cross a difficult concept to grasp. Even Christians are trying to find alternative ways of explaining it – some have abandoned the concept of atonement entirely.

Jesus, though, is far more than a victim. When God receives and approves the condemned Jesus he transcends the world of oppressor and victim to create a new humanity, capable of new kinds of relationships. Atonement speaks of a transition from brokenness, alienation and the death of love to a place of restoration, healing, and wholeness. A place that holds out hope for deepening friendships and mutual confidence - the exact same things the post-modern mind is lacking, and is looking for.

Paul Wells is Professor of Systematic Theology at Facult' Libre Theologie Reformee in Aix-en-Provence, France. He has been editor of La Revue réformée, a leading evangelical journal in French, since 1981. He is married to Alison who teaches adult English and they have three children who live in Spain and the English Midlands. Together they are involved in church planting in Gardanne, a mining town between Aix and Marseilles, where there is no other Protestant church.

JOHN BUNYAN

THE
INTERCESSION
CHRIST, A COMPLETE SAVIOUR
OF CHRIST

CHRISTIAN
HERITAGE

ISBN 978-1-84550-544-8

The Intercession of Christ

Christ, A Complete Saviour

JOHN BUNYAN

Biographical Introduction by William S. Barker. Bunyan wrote extensively on topical theological and practical matters, issues that faced the church in his time, which face us still. The Intercession of Christ is one of these works. In it Bunyan traces the nature of Jesus' intercession, who it should affect, the benefits it gives us and how effective that intercession is. Bunyan is also keen to show the interferences of the doctrine on such subjects as backsliding, how Christ's intervention is affected when we continue to sin, and there sins of God's people worse than the sins of others.

John Bunyan (1628-1688) was born the son of a metalworker near Bedford, England. He went on to become a famous preacher and writer and during his life penned over 2 million words, his most famous work being *The Pilgrim's Progress*.

MENTOR

THE LAMB
OF GOD
THE BIBLE'S UNFOLDING
REVELATION OF SACRIFICE

ROBERT L. REYMOND

ISBN 978-1-84550-181-5

The Lamb of God

The Bible's Unfolding Revelation of Sacrifice

ROBERT L. REYMOND

The central theme of Holy Scripture is the unfolding revelation of its doctrinal teaching on Jesus as the 'slain Lamb of God'. The doctrine of Jesus as God's slain lamb runs like a thick cable from Genesis to Revelation binding the entirety of Scripture together. Indeed Revelation 13:8 speaks of Jesus as the lamb who was slain from the creation of the world, while 1 Peter 1:19-20 speaks of the precious blood of Christ, a lamb without blemish or defect who was chosen before the creation of the world.

Reymond examines the biblical depictions concerning the Lamb of God – illuminating to us the central place that the suffering of the Messiah as God's lamb occupies in God's eternal purpose and earths history. Christ's Lamb work is to be found throughout the Old and New Testaments and its pivotal importance for each of our lives is explored in depth. Challenging, absorbing and full of spiritual nourishment Robert Reymond has produced a unique devotional study.

Robert L. Reymond taught for more than 25 years on the faculties of Covenant Theological Seminary (St. Louis, Missouri) and Knox Theological Seminary (Ft. Lauderdale, Florida). Currently he is the Emeritus Professor of Systematic Theology at Knox Theological Seminary, Ft. Lauderdale, Florida.

A CHRISTIAN'S POCKET GUIDE TO

JUSTIFI CATION

BEING MADE RIGHT WITH GOD?

GUY WATERS

ISBN 978-1-84550-615-5

A Christian's Pocket Guide to Justification

Being made right with God?

Guy Waters

Could you explain Justification if asked to? For many of us, the whole concept of justification is as mystifying as a foreign language, but yet Christians down the ages have fought to defend it – seeing it quite rightly as a vital element of how we are saved. But justification is not a relic of the past – it has direct relevance to us as Christians today. We often struggle with the thought of justification because of human pride; "I can't be that bad" and so justification is often undermined, wrongly presented or just plain ignored. Scripture though, is brutally clear: we have a real problem – the prospect of our lives marred by wrong-doing being laid out before an almighty God who is pure and will not forever let wrong go unpunished. We can't earn our way out of our predicament – as this is just "rubbish" according to the apostle Paul. We need something else, someone who can take the hit we so richly deserve – leaving us to be declared innocent instead. This little book will help you grasp a truth that when understood correctly is explosive, transformational and utterly liberating.

Dr Guy Waters is the Associate Professor of New Testament at the Reformed Theological Seminary, Jackson, Mississippi who has a particular interest in the letters and the theology of Paul. He is a teaching elder in the Mississippi presbytery of the Presbyterian Church of America.

Christian Focus Publications
publishes books for all ages

Our mission statement –

STAYING FAITHFUL
In dependence upon God we seek to impact the world through literature faithful to His infallible Word, the Bible. Our aim is to ensure that the LORD Jesus Christ is presented as the only hope to obtain forgiveness of sin, live a useful life and look forward to heaven with Him.

REACHING OUT
Christ's last command requires us to reach out to our world with His gospel. We seek to help fulfil that by publishing books that point people towards Jesus and help them develop a Christ-like maturity. We aim to equip all levels of readers for life, work, ministry and mission.

Books in our adult range are published in three imprints.

Christian Focus contains popular works including biographies, commentaries, basic doctrine and Christian living. Our children's books are also published in this imprint.

Mentor focuses on books written at a level suitable for Bible College and seminary students, pastors, and other serious readers. The imprint includes commentaries, doctrinal studies, examination of current issues and church history.

Christian Heritage contains classic writings from the past.

Christian Focus Publications Ltd,
Geanies House, Fearn, Ross-shire,
IV20 1TW, Scotland, United Kingdom
info@christianfocus.com
www.christianfocus.com